UNDERSTANDING THE IMPORTANCE OF INFORMATION

Beth A. Pulver and Donald C. Adcock

Heinemann
LIBRARY

www.heinemann.co.uk/library

Visit our website to find out more information about Heinemann Library books.

To order:

☎ Phone 44 (0) 1865 888066

📄 Send a fax to 44 (0) 1865 314091

💻 Visit the Raintree bookshop at www.heinemann.co.uk/library to browse our catalogue and order online.

Heinemann Library is an imprint of **Pearson Education Limited**, a company incorporated in England and Wales having its registered office at Edinburgh Gate, Harlow, Essex, CM20 2JE – Registered company number: 00872828

Heinemann is a registered trademark of Pearson Education Ltd.

Text © Pearson Education Limited 2008
First published in hardback in 2009
The moral rights of the proprietor have been asserted.

Edited by Andrew Farrow and Marta Segal Block
Designed by Richard Parker and Tinstar Design Ltd.
Picture research by Fiona Orbell and
    Elizabeth Alexander
Production: Alison Parsons

Originated by Chroma Graphics (Overseas) Pte. Ltd
Printed and bound in China by Leo Paper Group.

ISBN 978 0 431 90819 9 (hardback)
13 12 11 10 09
10 9 8 7 6 5 4 3 2 1

British Library Cataloguing in Publication Data
Pulver, Beth A.
   Understanding the importance of information. - (Information literacy skills)
   028.7

A full catalogue record for this book is available from the British Library.

Acknowledgements

The author and publishers are grateful to the following for permission to reproduce copyright material: © UK edition of "Memoirs of a Teenage Amnesiac" by Gabrielle Zevin, Bloomsbury Publishing Plc. p. 30; © Alamy pp. /Blend Images 10, /David Pearson 17; © Corbis pp. /Jeffry W. Myers 37, /Ed Kashi 19, /Henry Diltz 29, /Jonathan Brady/epa 41, /Reuters 21, /Underwood & Underwood 4; © Getty Images pp. /Akhtar Hussein/Liaison Agency 26, /Bruce Laurance 23, /Colourblind Images 5, /Indranil Mukherjee/AFP 12, /Ron Chapple/Taxi 11, /Valerie Macon/AFP 39; © Photodisc pp. 9, 38; © Photolibrary/Digital Vision 32; © The Library of Congress 6.

Background features and cover photograph reproduced with permission of © iStockphoto.

Every effort has been made to contact copyright holders of any material reproduced in this book. Any omissions will be rectified in subsequent printings if notice is given to the publishers.

Contents

Some words are shown in bold, **like this.** You can find the definitions for these words in the glossary.

The Importance of Information

Every day you receive thousands of pieces of information. Your parents, friends, and teachers all give you information. You read books, watch TV, surf the Internet, play video games, and listen to music. You are potentially getting information from all these activities.

If you have a question, whether it's something you want to know for your own interest or for a school project, you can research your answer in a number of places. Much of your research can be done very quickly **online** or in a library. If you don't have a book, you can find it at your school library, the public library, or a bookshop. If you can't get to any of those places, you can order it online without leaving your house.

With all these sources of information available, you probably take it for granted that you have the right to access information. In some parts of the world, people do not have the same access to information. In some countries the government limits the information people are allowed to have. In some places, even in this country, lack of technology, money, and other resources limit the information available.

In this book we will look at how our country's government and history support our right to information, and some of the responsibilities that come with the rights we have.

Andrew Carnegie donated the funds that allowed many libraries to be built.

Today libraries offer a variety of services, ranging from storytime for small children to providing tax forms for adults. They also provide computer and Internet access for many people.

Libraries and information

During the 18th and 19th centuries, many political, religious, and social leaders believed that a well educated public was necessary for a **democratic** society to flourish. They thought that for people to make good decisions, they needed as much information as possible.

Libraries play an important role in making information accessible. A free library gives everyone the same access to information, whatever their wealth or status. In Britain, the first town library under the control of local government was established in Norwich in 1608. In 1850, **Parliament** passed the Public Libraries Act and free lending libraries were opened in many towns and cities.

Later in the century, many libraries were built with funds donated by the Scottish-American businessman, Andrew Carnegie (1823–1929). Money from Carnegie built over 2,000 libraries around the world. More than 1,000 were in the USA, 660 in the UK, 156 in Canada, and 4 in Australia. Many of them are still in use today.

Types of library

There are many different kinds of library. A school library usually contains books at the right reading level for the pupils at the school. Your school library probably has fiction as well as non-fiction books. It may also have computers and other resources. Usually only pupils at the school are allowed to use the school library and borrow books from it.

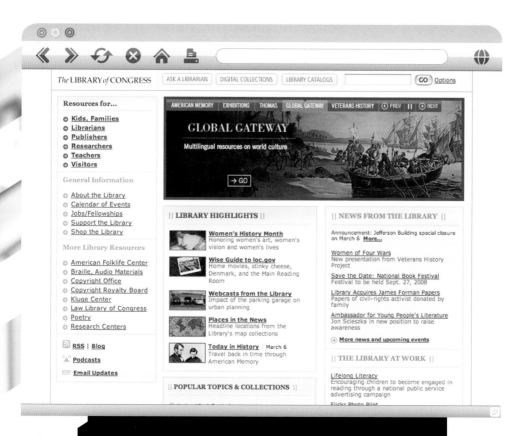

Today, with online catalogues, you can access libraries without leaving home.

Public libraries

A public library is usually run by a town or city. Most towns think it is important for local people to have access to information. Everyone is welcome at a public library, but usually only residents of the city or nearby cities can borrow books. Sometimes only residents of the city or nearby cities can use library resources such as computers. A public library may have a wide variety of fiction and non-fiction books, DVDs, CDs, and magazines. Some of these materials will be appropriate for you, but others will be too complicated or adult for your needs.

Some public libraries have a special children's area with comfortable chairs, and even toys. Some also organize events at which authors and other speakers give presentations on topics they are expert in. Some also have schemes where older boys and girls can volunteer to read to young children. Many public libraries hold book readings and local area meetings. Public libraries have all these resources because they exist to provide services to the local residents.

Special libraries

If you have a school project about architecture, you might look for books about the architect Sir Christopher Wren. You can probably find biographies of him, as well as books about his buildings, in your school or public library.

Imagine you are a historian studying architecture. You don't want to just read what other people say about Wren, you want to look at his designs yourself. You may even want to see his personal papers. This information may not be in a public library. It will probably be in a specialist library attached to a museum, or in a university library. Many famous people donate their papers to a specific library, for researchers to use in the future.

In a public library you can wander around looking at different books, but in many specialist libraries you have to ask the librarian for the book you want, and he or she brings it to you. These libraries often have very valuable books that must be kept safe for future research.

University libraries

Universities have very large libraries with thousands and thousands of books. They also have large collections of journals related to the subjects they teach. The major function of the libraries at universities is to provide the resources and assistance needed by the students and the staff who are conducting research. They may have a small collection of fiction books to read for pleasure, but the literature collection is provided for research purposes rather than reading pleasure. Many university libraries allow anyone to use their resources in the library, but only allow their students and teachers may borrow things from it.

Whatever kind of library you are using, the best way to find what you need is to start with a librarian.

The Right to Information

The right to freedom of information varies in different countries around the world. In the United Kingdom, individual freedoms have been built up over the centuries in a variety of legal documents and in **case law**. Recently the most important addition to Britain's "unwritten" constitution has been the codifying of the rights of individuals under the European Convention on Human Rights, which came into UK law as the Human Rights Act in 1998. In the United States, many individual freedoms are guaranteed by a written document, the U.S. Constitution, which became law in 1787.

Other countries have created a legal framework known as a Bill of Rights. This type of document protects individual freedoms. Most are based on the 1791 addition to the U.S. Constitution called the Bill of Rights.

From Article 10 of the Human Rights Act 1998

"Everyone has the right to freedom of expression. This right shall include freedom to hold opinions and to receive and impart information and ideas without interference by public authority and regardless of frontiers."

Freedom of speech

The Human Rights Act of 1998 has two sections, known as articles, which are important to people's right to information and free expression. In Article 9, everyone is guaranteed the "right to freedom of thought, conscience, and religion". Article 10 (see above) protects freedom of speech (see pages 42–43). This means that you cannot be arrested for speaking your mind, even if what you say disagrees with the government. Rights such as those in Articles 9 and 10 are not respected in many parts of the world, where governments want to control what people can say.

Limits on free speech

Having the right to speak your mind doesn't give you right to say whatever you want. You can still get into trouble with friends, parents, or teachers. There are other limits to this right, too. You are not allowed to lie about people. You cannot make false statements about a person that might damage their reputation. This is called **slander**.

Gossip is not protected under your right to free speech.

If you make up a story about someone, or write something that you cannot prove is true, and publish it in a newspaper or magazine, you can be taken to court for **libel**. You also cannot say something in order to cause a disturbance or riot. You may have heard the expression, "Like shouting 'Fire' in a crowded theatre." If you did this just to see what happened, you would be breaking the law, because such an act could be dangerous and cause a stampede. People could get hurt.

Freedom of the press

In many countries, the government controls the press. This means they own the newspapers and, in some cases, the radio and TV stations as well. In some places, those in power also try to control the Internet. They do this by blocking access to websites. Internet blocking is not just used by national governments. Individuals, companies, schools, and libraries can use software that prevents people from seeing selected websites.

In the UK, freedom of the press and media is protected by laws, including Article 10 of the Human Rights Act. Although the British Broadcasting Corporation (BBC) is funded by the national government, it is editorially independent. This means that the government cannot interfere in what is planned or broadcast.

In the United Kingdom, the freedom of the press protects all forms of news information.

Limits on press freedom

In most countries, there are limits on the freedom of the press. Just as is the case with freedom of speech, newspapers are not allowed to publish untrue stories or it is considered libel. Since the 1980s, laws have existed that mean **journalists** who have information that is considered to be vital to a police investigation can be forced to give evidence at a trial. In the last few years, two new laws have been passed that restrict the freedom

In the United States and many other countries, issues of freedom of speech and the press are often decided in courts.

of the press in the UK. After the bombings in London on 7 July 2005, the government passed the Prevention of Terrorism Act 2005. It includes **criminalization** of free speech when it contains "encouragements of terrorism". In 2006, the Racial and Religious Hatred Act became law. This makes it illegal to use the defence of freedom of the press to incite racial or religious hatred or violence.

The British press, and those who have supplied the press with information, have been taken to court by the government for using material protected under the Official Secrets Act. This act prohibits any disclosure of confidential material by government employees. Journalists who "come into the possession" of and repeat these disclosures are also considered to have broken the law.

Duties and responsibilities

Freedom of speech and freedom of the press allows everyone in a democratic society the chance to give their true opinions without fear of **reprisals** from those in power. Here in Article 10 of the Human Rights Act are some of the reasons why conditions and restrictions might be placed on freedom of expression "…in a democratic society":

- in the interests of national security
- in the interests of public safety
- for the prevention of disorder or crime
- for the protection of health or morals
- for the protection of the reputation or rights of others.

Other legal protections

By using the phrase, "right to the freedom of expression", Article 10 of the Human Rights Act also protects people's rights to perform, paint, or say on stage things that other people simply do not like or find offensive. It also protects other forms of communication. However, just because the Act protects a person's right to create controversial or unpopular works, it does not mean that a specific shop, museum, or theatre has to sell, display, or perform the works.

Is it censorship?

Newspapers cannot publish every story. Many stories are not well written, lack supporting proof, or would not be of interest to the newspaper's readers. There is not enough room in a newspaper or magazine to include every story. Editors and publishers are allowed to make decisions about what does and does not go in a newspaper or magazine.

Libraries and schools cannot afford to buy every book. Teachers, head teachers, and librarians all have to make decisions about which books to buy for the school. They buy books that are related to the subjects taught in their schools. Censorship and book banning does not refer to public places or businesses making reasonable decisions about which books they will and will not own.

Book banning

Despite your right to information, there are groups and individuals who wish to restrict access to certain material. This could be because they think it contains explicit or offensive language, unsuitable sexual content, violence, anti-religious content, or drug or alcohol use.

Groups sometimes try to keep others from reading books they do not approve of.

This happens most frequently where books for young people are concerned. A person or group of people may complain about a book or even attempt to get it removed from school classrooms, libraries, or bookshops. In most cases the reasoning behind the request for the removal of a book is that the individual or group believes the book could be offensive or harmful to a young person who reads it.

Cases of books being challenged

Over the last 25 years challenges have been made to a number of books. From nursery-level picture books to adult autobiographies, someone found the content in these books problematic:

Three Little Pigs This traditional children's story has been challenged in recent years because of its central characters. Schools with large numbers of Muslim pupils and libraries with many Muslim users have removed books with pig characters, which may cause offence to followers of Islam.

The *Harry Potter* books by J.K. Rowling have been condemned by many Christian groups and individuals. They see the stories as giving support to Satanism and other occult practices, such as magic. While fantasy books for young people have touched on these themes for many years, the phenomenal popularity of the *Harry Potter* books has made them a bigger target.

Spycatcher, Peter Wright's autobiography of his life as a British intelligence officer, was challenged in the courts by the UK government during the late 1980s. After getting publication of the book halted in the UK in 1985, it then attempted to stop publication in Australia, where Wright was living. The UK government lost this case in 1987 and the book came out in Australia and sold around the world, except in the UK. In June 1988, the UK government lost its last legal challenge to keep the book out of the country. It went on to sell more than two million copies.

King and King (by Linda de Haan and Stern Nijland), *And Tango Makes Three* (by Peter Parnell and Justin Richardson). In May 2008, several schools in Bristol withdrew these two children's picture books from their stocks after groups of parents challenged them because of the portrayals of same-sex couples. Some parents felt that it was not just the homosexuality that was inappropriate for the very young age-range involved, but any content that raised sexual issues.

The Da Vinci Code. This 2003 novel by Dan Brown was condemned by the Catholic Church for its portrayal of the Catholic Church and its institutions. Research undertaken by the Catholic Response Group in the UK found that the book had undermined people's trust in the claims of the Catholic Church. It had most seriously damaged the reputation of the *Opus Dei* organization. The Catholic Church was also very unhappy with the film made of the book.

Freedom of Information Act

The United Kingdom's Freedom of Information Act 2000 fully came into force on 1 January 2005. Scotland is covered by the Freedom of Information Act (Scotland) 2002 which came into effect on the same day. These Acts of Parliament introduce a "right to know" as regards the workings of public bodies. These bodies include government departments (central and local) the health service, schools and universities, the police, and other agencies, committees, and advisory bodies.

Features of the Freedom of Information Act 2000:

- There is no special format or form to use in making a request.
- Most requests will be handled for free. It is possible the person requesting the information will be asked to pay for photocopying or postage if relevant.
- Applicants do not need to give any reason for their request for information.
- Public bodies have 20 working days in which to respond to a request for information.
- Requests can be refused if it will cost more than £600 to collect the information requested, including the time spent searching for relevant files.
- Anyone can make a request. It does not depend on age, nationality, or where the person lives.

Over 120,000 requests for information are made each year, 60 percent from individuals, 20 percent from businesses, 10 percent from journalists, and the rest from other areas.

Other countries

Other countries also have Freedom of Information acts. Sweden's Freedom of the Press Act (1766) is thought to be the oldest. The U.S. Freedom of Information Act became law in 1966. This gives American citizens the right to information the government holds (national, state, and local). Any person or institution, such as a newspaper or a university, can request information. If the government does not want to provide the information, it needs to prove why the information cannot or should not be provided.

Many countries are currently developing similar laws. The pressure groups around the world that campaign for more freedom of information participate each year in "Right to Know Day" sponsored by the Freedom of Information Advocates Network.

A sample Freedom of Information Act request

Your name
Your address
Telephone number
email address

Date

Freedom of Information Act Officer
Address of public body you are contacting

Dear Sir or Madam

I would like to request copies of the following documents or any documents containing information about the following: [Now describe the information you are interested in. Be as clear and specific as possible giving as much detail as you can. For example, if you are aware that a decision about something you want to know about was made at a specific council meeting, ask for the minutes of that date, not just vaguely for information about the subject].

I understand that I may be required to pay a fee to cover the cost of photocopies and postage. I am willing to pay up to a maximum of £_____. If the fee payable is likely to exceed this limit, please let me know.

If you feel you must deny any part of this request, please give specific reasons for the refusal.

If you have any questions as regards my request for information, please contact me at the above telephone number or by email.

Thank you for dealing with my request.

Yours faithfully,

Your name

Why Is Equal Access to Information Important?

As the saying goes, "Knowledge Is Power." This is why non-democratic countries often try to limit the amount of information people have.

Democratic governments believe that for a democracy to be successful, its people should be well informed. Otherwise how can they participate in the decisions of the government? Information is needed not only for political decisions, but for everyday decisions as well. There are many things that can limit a person's access to information, including poverty and location. People in rural locations may be limited by a lack of electricity or libraries. Communities that have people living in poverty may have libraries and schools that are not funded well enough to provide access to many books and computers.

Consumer rights

Having limited access to information can cause a person to make bad decisions, or prevent them from getting further ahead in life. Consider a young woman buying her first car. She needs to know what type of car within her budget has the best fuel efficiency and safety record. She must also find out about car insurance. She wants to know which company offers the best coverage at a rate she can afford. Then she must find out the amount of road tax she will have to pay. All this requires hours of research and access to information, for the woman to make her decision.

Recommendations and evaluations

Unfortunately, there are dishonest organisations and businesses. Some businesses take people's money for services they do not perform. There are even fake charities that solicit money from people. It is important to carefully evaluate an organization or business before you give it your money.

In the United Kingdom, the Charity Commission is the regulator of all charities. It makes sure they operate properly. Consumer organizations such as Which? represent the interests of people using the goods and services provided by businesses.

One of the first steps in getting information about a business may be simply to talk to people you know. However, it is now very easy to spread false information about a business. For a small business this can be devastating.

Without the proper information, this woman could make a bad and expensive decision about her purchase. A skillful salesperson should help the customer with the information needed.

Health care

Access to information can make a difference for a person with a medical condition. Today, thanks to the Internet, people who are not medical professionals have access to a wide range of medical information. This can be both positive and negative. On the positive side, they can learn more about their medical conditions. They can join online support groups and talk to others with the same condition. If they are unhappy with their doctor, they can try to find a new doctor or more information online.

On the negative side, medical information can be difficult for non-professionals to understand. People may misdiagnose themselves based on information they do not understand. A person may decide he or she does not need to see a doctor, or does not trust the doctor, because of something they read online. When doing medical research, it is important only to use trustworthy sites and to discuss your findings with your doctor.

Voting

Access to information is important to voters during elections. Without access to information, people would not be able to have an educated say in their government. In a democratic country, it is important that information is available from a variety of sources. We have access to information about new laws and policies made by the government, our country's relations with other countries, and how our elected representatives are voting on the issues of the day. Without access to information, you would not know candidates' opinions on subjects such as wars, taxes, health care, immigration, and the environment. All this information means that you also have a responsibility to stay informed about the issues that are important where you live.

Gaining skills

The amount of information out there may seem overwhelming. But you already have many of the skills you need to evaluate and use it. Let's say you only have enough money to buy one CD this month. Your two favourite artists are both coming out with new releases. How do you decide which one to buy? Your best friend gives you her opinion, but you still aren't sure. You decide to do some research. You can read reviews in music magazines, read online reviews, or visit the shops and discuss it with the people working there. Even everyday purchases such as this can provide an opportunity to practise your research and evaluation skills.

The skill of evaluating information can be useful in all walks of life. These stockbrokers and traders often need to make quick decisions based on information that changes by the minute.

Government use of information

Individuals and businesses are not the only ones who need information. Governments need accurate information about their people and lands. Without this information, how can they decide where to build new schools, parks, and hospitals? Politicians need information about what people think on issues, so they can make fair laws and represent the voters' interests.

Censuses

One of the main ways a government gains information about its people is by conducting a census. A census is simply the counting of people in a specific area. The United Nations recommends that countries conduct a survey every ten years. In the United Kingdom the first census was held in 1801. A census is held every ten years. The information gathered helps governments to make decisions and predictions about the future.

Individuals and businesses have the right to view census information. This can help you if you are trying to do research about your family.

Privacy

Although the government needs to collect information about its citizens, individuals also have a right to privacy. The government needs to know how many people live in your house. However, it does not need to know what you talk about, where you go, what you eat, or what you think. Businesses also do not have the right to access all your personal information.

It is important to protect your right to privacy. This is why you should never give out personal information online. Often websites ask you to fill out surveys or answer questions. When you do this, you are giving information to the business running the site. You should always discuss such surveys with a trusted adult before filling them out.

Sometimes when you buy something in a shop, you are asked to give your post code or phone number. Shops do this to help them track where their customers live. However, you may be allowing the shop to call you, or to sell your phone number to others.

Countries around the world gather information about their citizens to use when making decisions. China employed more than 6 million census workers for its last nationwide census, in 2000. They gathered information about the country's population of 1.3 billion people.

Identity theft

One of the biggest security issues today is identity theft. This is when a person steals your personal information, such as your address, date of birth, and national insurance number. The person can use this information to open credit cards in your name. The thief never pays for the things they buy with these cards, in your name. It can take years to solve the problems created by identity theft. In the meantime, it may be difficult for you to obtain credit, or even get a job.

Pupils and information

As discussed before, children and young people also have rights to information. Schools need to develop programmes that provide access to information, and teach pupils how to use the information. Internationally, standards have been recommended for public and school libraries (see below). In many countries, the department in the national government in charge of education has rules or **"best practice"** standards for school libraries. There are also professional organizations, such as CILIP (Chartered Institute of Library and Information Professionals) and the SLA (School Library Association) in the UK, and the ALA (American Library Association) in the USA that campaign to improve school library provision.

The ILFA/UNESCO School Library Manifesto

The International Federation of Library Associations and Institutions (IFLA) and the United Nations Educational, Scientific, and Cultural Organization (UNESCO) have drawn up a document entitled "The School Library in Teaching and Learning for All", which lays out a number of things that all school libraries should aspire to as part of their **mission**. They should:

- Provide "information and ideas that are fundamental to functioning successfully in today's information and knowledge-based society".
- Provide resources that "enable all members of the school community to become critical thinkers and effective users of information in all formats and media".
- Provide services "equally to all members of the school community, regardless of age, race, gender, religion, nationality, language, professional or social status".
- Have staff that are adequately trained and funded, have materials, technologies, and facilities and be free of charge.

IFLA/UNESCO goals for a school library

The IFLA/UNESCO School Library Manifesto includes these goals for "the development of literacy, information literacy, teaching, and learning":

- Offering opportunities for experiences in creating and using information for knowledge, understanding, imagination, and enjoyment;
- Supporting all pupils in learning and practising skills for evaluating and using information, regardless of form, format, or medium, including sensitivity to the modes of communication within the community;
- Providing access to local, regional, national, and global resources and opportunities that expose learners to diverse ideas, experiences and opinions;
- Proclaiming the concept that intellectual freedom and access to information are essential to effective and responsible citizenship and participation in a democracy.

Adapted from the latest revision (March 2006) of the IFLA/UNESCO School Library Manifesto

Library skills and information literacy

This chart shows the "Seven Pillars Model". It has been developed by SCONUL to show the steps a learner needs to take to develop information literacy:

Basic Library skills and IT skills

1. Recognize information need
2. Distinguish ways of addressing the gap
3. Construct strategies for finding information
4. Find and access
5. Compare and evaluate
6. Organise, apply, and communicate
7. **Synthesize** and create

From the Society of College, National, and University Libraries

Information literacy skills will help learners develop habits that will make them independent researchers, investigators, and problem solvers.

School and public libraries

School and public libraries should be there to provide access to information and information technology. The information available in a school library needs to be developed, changed as necessary, and evaluated to support the school's curriculum and to meet the learning needs of all the pupils and staff. Just like public libraries, school libraries were developed to provide access to information for the whole school community. That right of access to information is an important intellectual freedom.

Although there are many school and public libraries throughout the world, some people still do not have access to information. Not every community has a public library. Not every school has a school library. There are people who live in areas so remote or so poor that Internet access is an impossibility. There are also still many places around the world where the government and politicians believe that not everyone is entitled to equal access to information.

What does a modern library provide?

- Books, books, and more books
- Homework and reference help
- Services for all members of the community
- Internet access
- Newspapers and periodicals
- DVDs and CDs
- Meeting places for groups and societies
- Activities and classes
- Local and family history information
- Art exhibitions.

The Responsibilities of Free Expression

As we discussed, freedom of expression is a right. This right is just as important as your right to access information. The right to free expression allows authors to write the information they think is important and have it printed, so that everyone can read it and learn from it. This right is given to everyone so that the exchange of ideas can be made freely. As citizens of a free society with an elected government, the right of free expression gives us the ability to make informed decisions about the election to government of our representatives, and government policy. With this right, however, comes great responsibility.

Your speech is protected, but this does not mean that you can say anything about anyone. Legally you are not allowed to speak false statements that might damage a person's reputation. This is called slander. You are also not allowed to write false statements that might damage a person's reputation. This is called libel. Both libel and slander are making false statements about a person, but one is done in speaking and one is done in writing. Both libel and slander are against the law.

The definition of slander and libel

The right to free expression does not include the right to make false statements about a person.

- Slander is when you make a false statement about a person that might damage their reputation. This statement is made orally.

- Libel is when you make a false statement in writing about a person that might damage their reputation.

- Both slander and libel are against the law.

A famous slander case

Oprah Winfrey has been a famous chat-show host in the United Staes for years. Her TV show is very popular, and she is seen as someone who can influence many people.

In April 1996, Oprah invited some people representing the beef industry and a vegetarian activist onto her show. There had recently been an outbreak of "Mad Cow" disease in the United Kingdom, and many people had concerns about the safety of eating beef. The two groups debated the safety of beef. As a result of the debate, Oprah Winfrey said that she would stop eating hamburgers.

In the state of Texas, USA there is a law that allows people to sue for libel or slander on behalf of a food or agricultural product. The beef industry claimed that Oprah's comments caused beef prices to fall dramatically. The courts ruled that, in fact, Oprah had not uttered any false statements. Oprah's right to free speech gave her the right to express her opinion about eating beef. After the trial, Oprah was quoted as saying, "Free speech not only lives, it rocks!"

Oprah Winfrey stands outside a Texas courthouse in 1998. What constitutes libel can be difficult to decide and may have to be determined in a court of law. The financial penalties for libel can be huge, but so can the costs of going to court.

Ironically, Oprah herself is often accused of limiting free speech. This is because she asks her employees to sign a very strict contract, which prevents them from discussing or writing about her for the rest of their lives.

Your responsibility

Today, with the Internet, it is very easy to spread false information. If you send an e-mail to a friend with a piece of gossip, that e-mail can be passed around the school before the next morning. You must think very carefully before putting information online. This is true of your personal information as well. If you put information on Facebook, MySpace, or other such sites, many people can look at it. Once information is posted online, it never really goes away. There have been cases of people losing their jobs because of e-mails they sent. There have even been cases of people losing their places on sports teams and job offers because of material they put on sites such as MySpace.

The right to gather

Related to your right to free speech is your right to gather as a group to discuss or protest about issues. Those who hold opinions different from yours also have this right. This right also must be used responsibly. You may need to ask permission to protest in a certain place at a certain time. You are not allowed to encourage your group or other groups to start a riot or fight with others who do not share your opinion.

As mentioned earlier, it is also good to be careful generally and not spread too much personal information around to too many people. Identity theft is a growing concern around the world. Computers assist us in many ways, but technology has also made it easier for criminals to steal people's identities and money.

Copyright laws

Protecting authors' freedom of speech goes further than allowing them to publish their ideas and opinions. It also means protecting those words, ideas, and opinions from being stolen. This protection is provided by the **copyright** law. The copyright law clearly says that an author's literary, artistic, musical, and dramatic piece of work is protected by the law. This means that in order to use it, you must ask the author's permission. It also means that you may not make copies or distribute duplicate copies to others. Artwork, the choreography of a dance, music, plays, and the staging of where the actors stand when performing the play are also protected by copyright law.

That means that you cannot perform another person's play, music, or choreography without his or her permission. Works of art such as paintings, sculptures, drawings, and photographs may not be reproduced without permission. Musical works, including the lyrics and music, are protected by copyright law. When you make a copy of your favourite CD to give to a friend, you may be breaking the copyright law.

A famous copyright case

George Harrison was a member of the pop group the Beatles. In 1970 he released a solo album. One of the songs, *My Sweet Lord*, was about Harrison's religious feelings. The song became a number-one hit. Many people thought the song sounded similar to a song from the 1960s, *He's So Fine*.

Harrison admitted that he had heard *He's So Fine* before, but said he had written his song independently, and that the two songs were different. The judge eventually ruled that while Harrison did not intend to copy *He's So Fine*, the two songs were almost identical. Harrison was found guilty of breaking the copyright laws. He took someone else's work, performed it as his own, and made money from it. Copying a song unintentionally is still breaking the copyright law. Money was awarded to the owner of the rights to *He's So Fine*.

Today, sampling is a popular music technique. Sampling refers to when an artist intentionally borrows a section from a famous song and includes it as part of his or her own song. People have different opinions as to whether sampling is a violation of copyright law or an example of **fair use**.

In the early 1970s, George Harrison was sued because his song *My Sweet Lord* sounded like a song by the Chiffons, *He's So Fine*. The judge ruled that Harrison had unintentionally copied the earlier song and had broken the law.

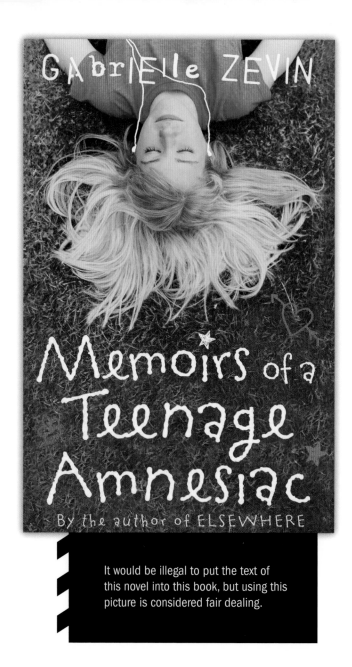

It would be illegal to put the text of this novel into this book, but using this picture is considered fair dealing.

Fair dealing

If you want to copy pages out of the encyclopedia to continue your research at home, you are not in violation of the copyright law. This is different from copying a CD, because you are using a small part of the whole book for research. This is allowed because of an exception in the law. This exception is called fair dealing. Fair dealing allows you to make copies of a certain amount of text, audio, or video for research and for education or discussion.

Amount of information use allowed under fair dealing

Most countries have laws that say how much of someone else's work an individual can use under fair dealing or fair use. In the United Kingdom this is covered under the Copyright, Designs, and Patents Act 1988 (CDPA). This act defines the term fair dealing as being "private study and criticism and review and news reporting".

Under the provisions of the CDPA, individuals are permitted to make a single copy for their own use of a "reasonable portion" for "research and private study" or "criticism, review, and news reporting" of literary, dramatic, musical and artistic works. However, nowhere is "reasonable proportion" explained or defined. Schools, colleges, and universities can also make special arrangements to pay for licences from the UK Copyright Licensing Agency in order to make multiple copies of portions of copyright material for educational use.

The *Harry Potter* books by author J.K. Rowling have been very popular for years. In 2008, Rowling sued a librarian who wanted to publish a dictionary, or mini encyclopedia, of the books. Rowling claimed that the book violated her copyright. The librarian claimed that the material used in the encyclopedia fell under the rules of fair dealing. Interestingly, the librarian first developed a fan website with the same information. Rowling did not object to the website, and even praised it, before the author tried to publish the information as a book.

Technology today

Today's technology, such as the Internet, databases, CD and DVD burners, digital video files, and digital sound files, make it very easy to violate the copyright law. When you make copies and sell or distribute them, you are in violation of the copyright law. This is called **piracy**. When you buy a CD or a sound file, it is for your use only. Copying the CD or a song from the CD and transferring that file to someone else's music player is illegal. However, it is legal to borrow CDs, books, and videos from a library.

Plagiarism

Just as you have the right to read works written by a variety of authors, the authors have the right to own and protect their work. **Plagiarism** is another word for cheating by copying. When you commit plagiarism, you submit someone else's ideas or words as your own.

Many people do this accidentally. They copy phrases or sentences from a book or article, forget where they found them, then copy them into their own work. Other people incorrectly believe that if they have changed the words around they have not committed plagiarism.

Catching plagiarism

Your teacher has many ways to find out if you have copied from someone else. If your work does not seem to be written by you, he will become suspicious. If you have copied from another pupil, past or present, the teacher may recognize the work or may ask other teachers if they recognize it. If you copy from a published source or something you find online, your teacher may type a few sentences into a search engine and discover that you have copied the work.

Most schools, colleges, and universities have strict rules against plagiarizing. In some places, plagiarising could lead to you being expelled or unable to graduate.

Most schools have strict rules against plagiarizing. The penalties may mean you fail the project or exam, or you may even be expelled, even if your plagiarizing was accidental. Adults have lost their jobs and the respect of other people as a result of committing plagiarism.

How to avoid plagiarizing

Take careful notes:

- Make sure you take notes as you read. Write down where you read something and what page it was on.
- If you copy a quotation from a book, be sure to mark it as a quotation.

Give credit where credit is due:

- If you agree with something you read in book, you can use a phrase such as, "As Jane Austen says... " This tells the reader who the thought belongs to.
- When writing your **bibliography** and footnotes, include more than is strictly necessary.

Use quotation marks:

- If you are quoting from a source, use quotation marks and make sure the sentence includes information about where you read the quote.

Protect yourself:

- Be sure to give yourself enough time to complete your project, that way you won't be tempted to take shortcuts.
- Keep drafts of your essay. Sometimes a pupil can be unfairly accused of plagiarizing. If you have copies of your notes and earlier drafts of your essay, you can prove that the thoughts are your own.

Citations

A bibliography, **footnotes**, and **endnotes** all help you to avoid committing plagiarism. As you are doing your research, make sure you list all your sources. This list will remind you which sources you might have paraphrased from or quoted to use in your work.

The list will also become your bibliography, or list of works **cited**. A bibliography is a list of each source used during research. Each citation for a type of source has its own format, but all contain basic information, including the author, title, publisher, and date of publication. Some source types, such as encyclopedia articles, magazine articles, and Web pages, require extra information for their bibliography entry.

Footnotes and endnotes

Footnotes are notes positioned at the bottom of the page. They refer to sources of information and include the page numbers where any quotes or paraphrases came from. When you see a number slightly above the last letter of a word, you will know that there is a footnote. An example might be if you read "bibliography.[1]" The number "[1]" would normally indicate that there is a note at the end of the page also labelled "1" that is related to a quote or paraphrase about a bibliography.

Endnotes also cite quotes or paraphrases used, but they are placed at the end of the work. Each note is in numerical order of use. Both footnotes and endnotes show that you have used information from reliable sources, and that the information is not your own work. Even though you have used footnotes or endnotes, you must also still include a bibliography in your work.

Today, many computer programs can help you create or manage footnotes or endnotes. Most word-processing programs, such as Microsoft Word, can do this. Professional researchers and writers often use programs designed specifically to keep track of citations and merge them into the main document.

A bibliography organizer

Create a grid, like this one, as your bibliography organizer. Fill in each section of the organizer as you use each information source. You will use this organizer to create your bibliography.

	Author	Source 1	Source 2	Source 3
Title of magazine, newspaper, or book				
Title of article				
Title of Web page				
Volume number				
Page numbers				
Edition number				
Publisher				
Copyright or update year				
Web address				
Date you first used website				

Fraud

As previously discussed, freedom of speech does not give you the right to lie about other people. You are also not allowed to commit **fraud**. Fraud is a legal term for lying in order to get something. Although you would hopefully never commit fraud, knowing the legal terms and rules gives you information that may help you make better decisions.

What is fraud?

Under UK law, there are three ways to commit a general offence of fraud:

- By false representation [lying].
- By failing to disclose information.
- By abuse of position [of power, privilege, knowledge, or control].

Someone can also commit fraud by obtaining services dishonestly, by making or supplying goods to be used in frauds, or by fraudulently trading or carrying on a fraudulent business.

Many fraud cases involve a person selling something. However, it is important to remember that certain things are allowed when selling. Let's say you go to a jumble sale. Someone wants to sell you a used video game. The seller says, "This game is awesome. It's the most fun, ever." Now, even if the seller hates the game, this is not fraud. It is not fraud because calling something "awesome" and "the most fun ever" are not statements of fact. They are simply **opinions**. Even if the seller hates the game, as a seller he is allowed to try to make it seem better than he believes it to be.

Let's say the seller tells you that the game is the newest version. He doesn't know that a newer version came out last week. This is not fraud because he is not intentionally lying. If the seller tells you that within one week of playing the game, your fingers will become so strong that you'll be able to lift a car, this is also not fraud. It is not reasonable for you to believe such an absurd statement.

This may sound pretty silly when talking about a video game. But imagine applying this information to a large purchase, such as a house or car. It is important to realise that as a consumer you have a responsibility to search out as much information as possible before making a decision. Your right to information comes with a responsibility to find the information you need.

Having information at your fingertips can protect you from fraud.

Information and Internet Freedom

The last 100 years have seen an explosion in information sources and means of obtaining and storing it. But even though we have new technology, we have the same rights to information, and the same need for our freedoms to be protected. Sometimes it is a challenge for the law to keep up with the pace of change, especially since the Internet doesn't respect international boundaries.

The Council of Europe Convention on Cybercrime

At the beginning of the 21st century, the Council of Europe (COE) drafted and then approved (in November 2001) a treaty to fight **cybercrime** (see page 43). Since it came into force in 2004, over 40 countries, including many in Europe, the United States, and Canada have signed and ratified it. International treaties, like the Convention on Cybercrime, only become legal in a place when a national government signs and ratifies the treaty, making it a part of that country's national law.

The Convention states that countries that ratify its provisions must pass laws similar to those it contains. The Convention covers regulations on

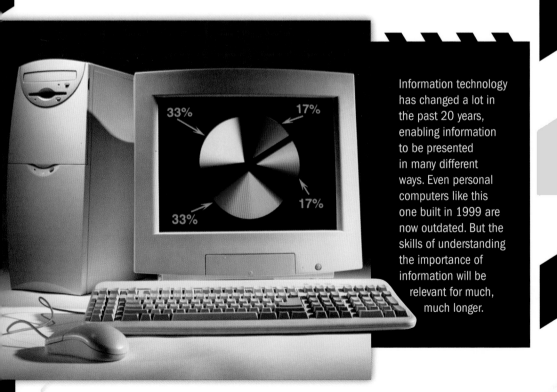

Information technology has changed a lot in the past 20 years, enabling information to be presented in many different ways. Even personal computers like this one built in 1999 are now outdated. But the skills of understanding the importance of information will be relevant for much, much longer.

In 2007, writers of TV programmes and films in the USA went on **strike** to get a better contract. Many broadcasters show programmes on the Internet. The writers wanted to ensure they were fairly paid when their work went online. This is an example of how copyright and free speech issues are developing and changing.

many aspects of computer and Internet-based crime, including:

- criminal laws against hacking
- laws relating to copyright infringement
- laws on Internet child pornography
- laws on computer-related fraud
- laws against using computer networks to publish racist and **xenophobic** material.

Parts of the Convention will make it easier for countries to work together to fight cybercrime. There are provisions for the interception and seizure of illegal communications, arrest of those involved, and their **extradition**. The UK has signed, but not yet ratified the Convention.

Are new laws a risk to Internet freedom?

Some people are worried about civil **liberties** and think that more laws to control the Internet, like the COE Convention, will limit freedom to information, However, many of the crimes committed using the Internet are already prohibited by laws against other media, such as theft and fraud. Should a criminal get away with it just because he or she used the Internet?

Summary

Democratic governments believe it is important for people to have access to information and the freedom to express their opinions. The 21st century is considered the age of information. At no time in history has so much information been so easy to access. We are surrounded by information at home, at school, and in our communities. Information comes from many sources such as books, magazines, newspapers, databases, the Internet, food packaging, instruction manuals, and the directional or advertising signs all around us.

We all have questions or problems to solve. Some are part of a school project. Others are the result of our own curiosity. Everyone should be able to find the answers to questions or solutions to problems. Not everyone has the good fortune to have the same access to information. Access to information is often determined by income and location. People with a limited income may not be able to afford to buy books and magazines, let alone computers. To have access to information, some people must rely on public or school libraries. However, they may not have access to such places, if they live in very remote locations. These places may have no running water, electricity, or telephone services. Some communities do not have a public library, and some schools do not have a library, so the people there have limited or no access to information.

Your rights and responsibilities

Your rights to access information are protected by laws. The creators of information are also protected by laws. They are protected by copyright and trademark laws. According to these laws, you may not use information from an author or artist as your own without permission. By using quotation marks, endnotes, footnotes, and bibliographies, you are giving credit to the authors and artists who created the information you are using. When you do not give credit to the source of your information and use it as your own, this is a form of cheating called plagiarism.

While today's new technology has created new issues, your basic right to obtain information, and your responsibility to use that information fairly and wisely, has not changed.

Sources of information have changed rapidly, including the ability to access it on touch screens on mobile phones. Yet understanding the importance of that information and making sure it is used properly is a skill that will always be useful.

The Human Rights Act 1998

"Article 9

Freedom of thought, conscience and religion

1 Everyone has the right to freedom of thought, conscience and religion; this right includes freedom to change his religion or belief and freedom, either alone or in community with others and in public or private, to manifest his religion or belief, in worship, teaching, practice and observance.

2 Freedom to manifest one's religion or beliefs shall be subject only to such limitations as are prescribed by law and are necessary in a democratic society in the interests of public safety, for the protection of public order, health or morals, or for the protection of the rights and freedoms of others.

Article 10

Freedom of expression

1 Everyone has the right to freedom of expression. This right shall include freedom to hold opinions and to receive and impart information and ideas without interference by public authority and regardless of frontiers. This Article shall not prevent States from requiring the licensing of broadcasting, television, or cinema enterprises.

2 The exercise of these freedoms, since it carries with it duties and responsibilities, may be subject to such formalities, conditions, restrictions, or penalties as are prescribed by law and are necessary in a democratic society, in the interests of national security, territorial integrity, or public safety, for the prevention of disorder or crime, for the protection of health or morals, for the protection of the reputation or rights of others, for preventing the disclosure of information received in confidence, or for maintaining the authority and impartiality of the judiciary."

Council of Europe Convention on Cybercrime Treaty

"Open for signature by the member States of the Council of Europe and by non-member States, which have participated in its elaboration, in Budapest, on 23 November 2001. Entry into force: 1 July 2004.

Official Summary of the Convention

The Convention is the first international treaty on crimes committed via the Internet and other computer networks, dealing particularly with infringements of copyright, computer-related fraud, child pornography and violations of network security. It also contains a series of powers and procedures, such as the search of computer networks and interception.

Its main objective, set out in the preamble, is to pursue a common criminal policy aimed at the protection of society against cybercrime, especially by adopting appropriate legislation and fostering international co-operation.

The Convention is the product of four years of work by Council of Europe experts, but also by the United States, Canada, Japan and other countries which are not members of the Organization. It has been supplemented by an Additional Protocol making any publication of racist and xenophobic propaganda via computer networks a criminal offence."

Glossary

best practice best way to do something that all involved should aspire to

bibliography list of sources used in researching a topic

case law laws built up over time based on the decisions of judges in court cases

censor delete information

cite list as a resource

civil liberties fundamental rights guaranteed by law, such as freedom of speech

copyright protection given to an author or artist against copying in any form without the permission of the author or artist

criminalization making something into a crime through legislation

cybercrime crimes committed over the Internet or using a computer

democratic related to a government controlled by the people

endnote note placed at the end of a work that gives the source of a quote or paraphrase of information from a resource used in writing the work

extradition sending someone from one country to another to stand trial

fact something that can be proven to be true

fair dealing part of the copyright law that allows a person to use portions of a work for educational or other purposes without the creator's permission

footnote note placed at the bottom of the page of a work that gives the source and page of a quote or paraphrase of information from a resource used in writing the work

fraud intentional lie told to trick someone

journalist person whose job is to write or edit for the print or broadcast media

libel false statement made about a person in writing that damages that person's reputation

mission goals of a specific programme, duty, or task

online connected to or available through a computer system

opinion statement of belief

Parliament national law-making assembly of the United Kingdom. It is made up of the House of Commons and the House of Lords.

piracy stealing; usually referring to copying electronic information, such as a CD or DVD

plagiarism using the ideas or words of another person as one's own

reprisal act of retaliation in punishment for something

slander spoken false statement that damages the reputation of a person

strike organized stop of work so that a group of workers has more power to negotiate

subscription library library that requires a membership fee to join or payment to take out books

synthesise put together or combine

xenophobic expressing hatred for those of a different nationality, or from a different region

Find Out More

Books

Just the Facts: Cyber Crime, Neil McIntosh (Heinemann Library, 2002)

Behind the News: Internet Freedom, Jane Bingham (Heinemann Library, 2007)

Websites

www.freedomhouse.org
Freedom House is an independent civil rights monitoring body that publishes annual reports, by country, on press and media freedom around the world.

www.cpbf.org.uk
The Campaign for Press and Broadcasting Freedom is a UK-based body that campaigns for press and media freedom.

www.ifex.org
The International Freedom of Expression Exchange is a global network of 70 non-governmental organizations that promotes freedom of the press and freedom of expression.

www.sla.org.uk
This is the website of the School Library Asociation (SLA). It has links to information about the purpose and use of school libraries.

http://copyright service.co.uk
This website of the UK copyright service gives advice based on the latest UK copyright law.

Disclaimer

All the Internet addresses (URLs) given in this book were valid at the time of going to press. However, due to the dynamic nature of the Internet, some addresses may have changed, or sites may have changed or ceased to exist since publication. While the author and publishers regret any inconvenience this may cause readers, no responsibility for any such changes can be accepted by either the author or the publishers. It is recommended that adults supervise pupils on the Internet.

Further Research

Now that you know about your right to information, exercise it! Practise your research skills by researching some of the topics mentioned in this book.

Freedom of Information Act
Look at the information on the Freedom of Information Act (pages 14–15). What countries do and do not have similar laws? Are any countries currently considering creating such laws?

Copyright
Look at the information on famous copyright cases (pages 30–34). See if you can find copies of both "He's So Fine" and "My Sweet Lord". Do you think the two songs sound alike? What was the final decision in the J.K. Rowling case?

Fraud
Look at the information on fraud (pages 38–39). Recently, several cases of literary fraud have occurred, including fake memoirs and news stories. How do these things happen? Why do people write these fake stories?

Websites
Which countries around the world grant their citizens the right to information? Which do not? What do the two groups of countries have in common?

Index